NOW YOU CAN READ. . . .
PETER AND JOHN
AT THE BEAUTIFUL GATE

STORY RETOLD BY LEONARD MATTHEWS

ILLUSTRATION BY GWEN GREEN

Published by Rourke Publications, Inc., P.O. Box 3328, Vero Beach, Florida 32964. Copyright © 1984 by Rourke Publications, Inc. All copyrights reserved. No part of this book may be reproduced in any form without written permission from the publisher. Printed in the United States of America.

The Publishers acknowledge permission from Brimax Books for the use of the name "Now You Can Read" and "Large Type For First Readers" which identify Brimax Now You Can Read series.

Library of Congress Cataloging in Publication Data

Matthews, Leonard.
  Peter and John at the Beautiful Gate.

  (Now you can read—Bible stories)
  Summary: Retells the Bible story in which Peter and John healed the lame man at the gate of the Temple.
  1. Bible stories, English—N.T. Acts.   [1. Bible stories—N.T.]   I. Title.   II. Series.
  BS551.2.M37   1984   226'.609505   84-15138
  ISBN 0-86625-314-9

GROLIER ENTERPRISES CORP.

NOW YOU CAN READ.....

PETER AND JOHN
AT THE BEAUTIFUL GATE

Easter had passed. Jesus had gone back to Heaven. He left behind Him His faithful followers. They had to carry on the good work that He had begun. One day Peter and John went walking together. They came to the Temple of Jerusalem.

At the entrance to the
Temple there stood a gate.
It was so grand that it
was known everywhere as
the Beautiful Gate.
At the side of the gate
there sat a beggar.

The beggar was lame. He had never walked in his life. Every day he was carried to the Beautiful Gate by his friends. As Peter and John passed him he called out to them.

"Please give me something," he cried.

Peter and John stopped. Peter spoke.

"Look at us," he said. The beggar
looked up into the kind faces of the
two men. He held out his bowl. He
hoped they would put some money in it.
It was easy for Peter to understand
what the man was thinking.

Peter shook his head. "No," he said.
"I have no money to give you. Instead,
I will give you something else."
The lame man shrugged his shoulders.
He needed money.
Peter smiled. He reached down and
took the beggar's hand.

"In the name of Jesus, stand up and walk," Peter said quietly. Suddenly there was a strange feeling in the lame beggar's legs. They became strong! He could not believe what was happening. Peter pulled his hand.

"Stand up," he said again. The beggar moved his legs. Then, slowly but without help, he got to his feet.

"I can stand! I can stand!" he shouted with joy. He was so happy.

"Now walk," said Peter. The beggar
moved one foot forward. Carefully,
he took his weight from that foot.
He moved the other foot forward. Then
he took several steps. He could walk!
He who had never walked could
now walk.

"God be praised!" cried the beggar. "I can walk!" Peter and John smiled at each other as the beggar ran off, shouting at the top of his voice.

A crowd of people began to gather.

"Another miracle!" said one of them. "Nonsense!" said another. He looked at Peter. "How did you make the lame man walk?" he asked.

"By the power of Jesus," said Peter.

At once the crowd began to talk among themselves. "Those two are the friends of that man Jesus," they said.

The man who had spoken to Peter hurried to tell the priests in the Temple what had happened.

"And the men who helped the lame beggar walk were friends of Jesus," he gasped. The priests had been the enemies of Jesus.

"This is not good news," said one. "When Jesus died, we thought that would be the end of Him. Now, here are His friends stirring up trouble for us. We must stop them."

"How are we to do that?" asked
another priest.

"Put them in prison," replied the
chief priest. "It is the only way."
The order to imprison Peter and
John was given. Soldiers found them
and took them to prison.

Peter and John, those two faithful friends of Jesus, were thrown into a dark cell.

Meanwhile, word of their capture spread quickly. Many people still remembered Jesus and how He had helped them. They did not like to think that two of His friends were in prison.

The next morning Peter and John looked through the bars of their cell. Outside, a great crowd had gathered. The people were angry.

"Release Peter and John!" they shouted. The priests were scared.

"The people will attack us if we do not release Peter and John," said one of the priests.

The chief priest sent for all the powerful enemies of Jesus. They were the men who had sent Jesus to the cross. They wanted to speak with Peter and John.

Peter and John were taken from prison and brought before the priests.

"From where did you get the power to cure a lame beggar?" asked the chief priest. Peter used the words he had spoken the day before.

"By the power of Jesus," he said. The priests frowned. Peter stood before them bravely. He had not always been brave. When Jesus had been taken prisoner, His enemies had asked Peter if he was a friend of Jesus. Three times Peter had said "No."

Later he had been ashamed. Now, he was brave and proud to be known as a friend of Jesus.

"Only by the power of Jesus could the lame beggar be cured," Peter said again. "Only by His power can we all be saved." Outside the crowd was shouting louder than ever. The chief priest thought. What should he do?

There was only one thing he could do.
He would have to please the people.

"I will set you both free," he said. "You will stop speaking about Jesus. If you do not, you will both be punished."

So Peter and John were set free. Bravely, however, they never stopped speaking about Jesus.

All these appear in the pages of the story. Can you find them?

chief priest

Peter and John

the beautiful gate

the beggar

soldier

Now tell the story in your own words.